This story is dedicated to the generations of caring parents who take the time to shape our imaginative leaders of tomorrow by reading them bedtime stories today. My lessons shared in this book were taught to me by my loving parents, my three children, and are still being reinforced by my three precious grandchildren everyday.

Love, "POP" / Hal

THE BEAR ESSENTIALS™
Book One of the Eli Bear Stories Series
Published by Heroic Hearts Media, LLC®
Carpinteria, CA USA

Written by Hal Price
Book Designed by Michael Bayouth

Copyright © 2019 by Hal Price
First Edition, September 2019
Author services by Pedernales Publishing, LLC
www.pedernalespublishing.com
ISBN 978-0-9833562-4-0 Hardcover Edition
ISBN 978-0-9833562-5-7 Paperback Edition
ISBN 978-0-9833562-6-4 Digital Edition
Library of Congress Control Number: 2019911893
Printed in the United States of America

All rights reserved. This book may not be reproduced in whole or in part, in any form (beyond copying permitted by Sections 107 and 108 of the United States Copyright Law, and except limited excerpts by reviewer for the public press), without written permission from Hal Price or his heirs. For information or bulk purchases please email: HalPrice@EliBearStories.com

Eli Bear Stories:

Written by Hal Price

Illustrated by Michael Bayouth

First Edition, September 2019

Published by: Heroic Hearts Media, LLC Carpinteria, CA USA
© 2019 by Hal Price www.EliBearStories.com

There's a story every father bear
Shares with his sweet young cub.
They tell them at the perfect time
When their cub needs special love.

Eli Benjamin Bear was very sad.
His Dad was leaving town.
Eli begged his father not to leave,
He wanted him around.

Eli's father then looked down and said.
"Son, I have to leave tonight.
I can sit here while you fall asleep.
Then turn out your bedroom light."

Eli Benjamin Bear began to pout.
He pitched a little fit.
He turned his back on Daddy Bear
Saying, "If I had your job, I'D QUIT!"

Eli's father cried a little tear
(That Eli did not see).
"I am sorry that you feel that way
Your sadness saddens me."

Eli's Father stroked his young son's head
Saying, "Son, I can't unpack."
He stroked his angry little head
and said, "I'll be right back!"

He said, "I have a gift for you.
My Papa gave to me.
Like you, I was an angry bear
So mad, I could not see!

"Papa said he wrote this letter
For the times we feel apart
To remember we are always loved
And connected by our heart.

"This letter is so special
I've kept it locked indoors.
By the time you wake tomorrow,
This letter will be yours!"

Eli snuggled tightly with his Dad.
He'd never felt so close.
He heard his Dad's heart beating strong.
(That's the sound he loved the most.)

"Papa called it BEAR ESSENTIALS
Ways to live life from your heart."
He looked at Eli lovingly
And said, "Relax son, now let's start:

"Be who you are and know yourself.
Pretenders are not real.
Say what you mean and don't hold back.
Express the way you feel.

"When you know yourself you can't be lost
And your life will take you far.
The key is being TRUE TO YOU
And remembering who you are!

"Respect all life, it's here for you
And trust your heart to guide.
Know love surrounds you every day.
It never leaves your side.

"Be still and quiet, you're not alone.
And in your stillness hear
The whispers of your heart's wise voice
That cares for you, my dear.

"Please, laugh and sing out every day.
Your joy expressed in sound
Can fill the hearts of those you love.
They're blessed when you're around.

"Remember, every word and thought
Creates the world you'll see.
And say 'I Love You' every day...
And say it joyfully!

"Remember, you are special child
And have a precious gift,
And when you bring your gift to serve
The hearts you touch will lift.

"One final message for you now,
Its power will ring true.
I believe in you with all my heart,
Now, YOU believe in YOU!"

Eli's Dad leaned down to kiss his head
Saying, "I love you and your heart.
You are my greatest gift of love
I have felt it from the start."

Eli Bear then asked his father,
"Will you love me while you're gone?"
His father smiled and kissed his head saying,
"I will love you ALL LIFE LONG!"

Father Bear tucked Eli's blanket snug
And turned the nightlight on.
He watched his bear cub fall asleep...
And the next day he was gone.

Their two hearts were connected now.
Eli kept Dad inside his heart.
Eli felt his father's love for him.
Now they'd never be apart.

Eli woke up feeling special.
His heart felt special too.
He heard his heart say quietly,
"Eli Bear, I sure LOVE YOU!"

Eli's heart beat softly as it said,
"There are things I'd like to share.
About how special you are now,
You are not an average bear!"

"It is true, your heart can speak to you!
It can help you find your way.
There are secret ways to listen.
You can trust what it will say.

"It can teach you how to listen
It can teach you how to hear
It can teach you why you're special
It is always very clear."

Eli Bear got so excited
He had a new best friend.
He could ask his heart for guidance
He could ask things without end.

Eli thought about so many things
Where would his questions start?
He sat quietly on his bedside
And placed his hand upon his heart.

Now You Can Ask Your Heart Questions Just Like Eli!

You Just Have To Ask, Feel, Listen And Then Either Draw A Picture Of What You Hear Or Write It Down.

To See Eli's Questions, Go To:

www.elibearstories.com/myheartsquestions

HAL PRICE
The Author

MICHAEL BAYOUTH
The Illustrator

Hal is the 2018 "Mindfulness" award-winning author of the best-selling book, *The Adventures of Eli Benjamin Bear: A Heart's Journey Home.* His books teach readers how to listen to the wisdom of their hearts and are currently being used as a curriculum in many public schools for Social-Emotional Learning. He donates a portion of the sale of each book in support of Teddy Bear Cancer Foundation's fight against Pediatric Cancer.

Prior to discovering his passion for writing stories, Hal worked for 40-years for two Fortune 100 companies as a marketing executive. In 2014, Hal had a "heart awakening" that redirected his life's purpose. He now uses his gift of writing and telling stories to inspire others to seek and live their purpose by following their own heart's guidance.

Michael makes a living as a freelance artist focusing in such areas as illustration, graphic design, fine arts, storyboarding, sketching, filmmaking and writing. Bayouth has worked in the entertainment field his whole life. He was the graphic designer on *The Office*, and for *The Orville* he storyboarded the first 2 seasons. He also created the DVD cover art for many of Disney's signature classics. His in-depth knowledge of typography, graphic design and illustration come from years of working with Disney, Stan Lee and the majors in Hollywood. He's also an author and an award-winning filmmaker. He attended Art Center College of Design.

He currently resides in Ventura, California where he freelances illustration and graphic design.
www.bayouthproductions.com

www.elibearstories.com

www.bayouth.com

www.ingramcontent.com/pod-product-compliance
Lightning Source LLC
Chambersburg PA
CBHW040731020526
44112CB00058B/2934